Play

poems by

Kristina Nichole Brodbeck

Finishing Line Press
Georgetown, Kentucky

Play

ACKNOWLEDGMENTS

"Imprint," *The Cape Rock*
"Clay and Hips and Jungles," *Calliope*
"Water Calls," *Calliope*
"Bad Mother" (2), *For a Better World* 2017

Thank you to the English departments at NKU and MSJU for the roles
you have played in supporting, encouraging, and reading this project. In
particular, thank you to Professor Kelly Moffett, for directing this project in its
thesis format, and to Dr. Elizabeth Mason and Professor Jeff Hillard for their
unwavering support. Thank you Dr. Emily Detmer-Gobel and Dr. Jessica
Hindman for serving as readers for this collection in its thesis format. Thank
you Carola and Lynn for reading, supporting, and loving. Thank you, my
dear Ryan. Thank you Jennie, my sister and who for so long was our mother's
primary caretaker.

Publisher: Leah Maines
Editor: Christen Kincaid
Cover Art: Ryan Brodbeck
Author Photo: Ryan Brodbeck
Cover Design: Leah Huete

Printed in the USA on acid-free paper.
Order online: www.finishinglinepress.com
          also available on amazon.com

Author inquiries and mail orders:
Finishing Line Press
P. O. Box 1626
Georgetown, Kentucky 40324
U. S. A.

Table of Contents

Six

Seven

To Theresa, and to all mothers forgetting and forgotten.

One

Suffocate

I wrap your foot in a bandage after you've kicked a hole in the door.
In the refrigerator I've made you a nighttime sandwich.
The laundry room door is shut, to keep you from layering laundry throughout the
    living room.
Closets have been emptied, cleaning supplies set on top shelves, the stove unplugged.

I tuck you in, whisper goodnight. Asleep, you look like you could remember.

The door to your condo locks on the outside,
so the streets won't take you again.

Rush

Tonight after you fall asleep I decide to escape you.

I park the car in the furthest spot in the parking lot and sit for a few moments
in the dread of you locked inside, even that will no longer keep you safe.
You'll have to go, and you'll have to go soon.

When I start to see the scene of leaving you in a nursing home, the moment
when I will tell you, *no you can't come with me, you have to stay now*,
my breath quickens,
but we aren't there yet.

Minutes later I step into the waiting room of the restaurant and my husband
asks where the baby is. And I realize we've been *there* for months now,
and I've been lying to the son, to the husband, to the sister, to you,
to the baby I forgot in the car.

I sprint just to find her sleeping, not knowing all we've learned to forget together.

After You Were Found on Lyness Street

Today I came home with a tracking device for your wrist. You were lost yesterday, on a sidewalk two streets away. The neighbors found you and called the police. The police told me about a program for this tracking device, so I signed the paperwork and wrote the check today. This act filled with self-pity, wondering about the legal ramifications of leaving you alone again. If you set fire to the condo unit, and a neighbor was killed—would I go to jail? You're still on the waiting list for a nursing home, but you're not bad enough to be a priority. We have to wait for you to seriously hurt yourself or another, or at least almost.

I had to talk you into sitting down and to let me lock the bracelet. I found you later in the bathroom, speaking to the mirror.

My husband won't stand for this. He won't. My husband is a doctor. His name is Charles and he's a doctor. I don't do drugs. I told them I don't do drugs. Laura said she is going to keep me here. This is my goddamn house. Laura says it's her house but it's my goddamn house. I paid for it.

I watched you talk to yourself in the mirror for a while, I don't know who Laura is, you don't have a husband anymore and his name wasn't Charles. Why is this happening? This can't be simply Alzheimer's. Maybe it's schizophrenia. I walk into the kitchen and type a message to my husband, telling him what's happening—he has no solution. Suddenly, you're in the living room again, just a few feet from me, wandering. You're picking up laundry you had scattered on the surfaces and moving each piece to a new home. This moment is similar to watching a preschooler engaged in imaginary play, that moment when you would look to your spouse and say, *Don't you just wish you knew what was happening in her head right now?*

Two

Before the St. James Church Remodel

When I return to my mother's church, I sit in the pew where she had sat.
Soon, it will all be torn away. Maybe those plaster walls trapped her breath.

I love tiled counter tops and gold finishings—
        it's what my mother would have seen as she mothered,
before her home prematurely emptied like this church.

My children know I'm an imposter,
but they have no choice.

As I leave, I brush my palm on the door handle before the walk home
along the fence where her grave should be.

Cause of Death: Assault

My children imagine their lives without me as their mother.

At the dining room table, they draw pictures of their new mother. I hear,
The new mama will be real, and our new house will be huge and white.

   I often mourn for the wives who suffer and then throttled by divorce filings,
   unfaithful husbands, and step moms to their children.

And as I write this, I wonder where the man is that I would leave my children for—
with so many wives and husbands leaving,
there's that person we would all do that for, right?

That man walks past our home, leaves a card, then waits.

Death by Miscarriage

In a turquoise room, a turquoise floor
holds my brain.

I want to keep my blue child safe just below my sweater
next to the diamond from my father's wedding band
that's pierced into my belly.

I often think of the child my parents lost
in the photo of my father and mother,
I trace both of their lips with my smallest finger.

Decipher

I don't know where you end, and where your ghost begins.

> You seep into me as I ride on the streets you drove,
> and your scream comes from the home
> where you raised me.

> I pass the repaved sidewalks where you walked,
> but because of city improvements, they no longer
> hold your footprints,

You've become your wheelchair. I kiss your hands,
> try to apologize.

Eating

When researching ways not to forget my children, I thought that becoming a vegan would save me from memory loss. I was stuck on how it would feel to forget them. To have my children come to visit my mediocre nursing home and I wouldn't know them. I'm sure, this likely feels like nothing. I would likely feel joy from their faces that look just like mine, but I wouldn't know what my face looks like anymore, so I wouldn't draw that conclusion. I would feel the same joy from them as I would feel from the tattooed nurses aid speaking to me the way I speak to my twenty-two month old baby daughter now. The joy for my children would no longer be exclusively for them. I'd forgotten them and I would respond to the bright voices of anyone who speaks to me in a certain pitch and tone with a smile. I kept researching veganism. It seemed to be the way to save myself from everything—cancer, forgetting, failing marriage, sin. This eating meat could be the root of anxiety and disease. Since I always feared eating pigs, it wouldn't be a leap. I thought I would just have to continually think of the babies and mothers separated in order to not fill my plate with meat. This worked for a while. It became a method of respect for the mothers and babies' establishment. I would think of the mother chicken never getting to hatch her eggs, of the baby chicks hatched under lights and then ground into feed if they were born male, of the mother cow never getting to nurse her calf so we can have chocolate chip and rocky road ice creams, and the male calf turned into veal. This was easy. Remembering not to eat meat or cheese became easy. I turned my attention to making my mother remember me. I spent days holding my newborn daughter on my mother's lap in her wheelchair. I couldn't let go because my mother would surely drop her. This will make her remember, I thought. I wondered, too, what the mother hog have thought after her babies were taken from her? The smallest ones broken over the concrete while she listened, trapped in a nearby pen. How long does she remember these babies? She's surely had droves of piglets in her short life. Does she know that the smallest ones will perish first? Does it matter, since they are all destined to become part of the ceramic stage of our dinner plates? If given the chance, would she throw herself in front of a pickup truck, womb full of fetal piglets, to save herself, to save them?

Mirror

A mirror walks in. It holds you with the man,
—not your husband or the father of your children but the doctor
you would have met had you chosen him, not us.

A new one sits in your place now. She holds
the grandchildren and his hand. She found
them after wading through the lake of sleeping embryos,
pushing yours aside with a wooden oar.

And here I sit, under deadened roots, clinging to my books,
waiting to crawl inside the pages, to live there.

Manner of Death: Dissolution

I've been fucking your husband her email reads, without apology.

The wife sleeps in these words.

> It's this notion of marriage that isn't covered in the pre-Cana sessions,
> a spouse has the power to throttle the other with indifference.
>
> It's where the partnership turns into a hunt, the desire to win
> by being the first to find another outweighs the desire to repair damage.

This relationship ends, with burned photo canvasses
piled by the curb.

Noon

I build a greenhouse in a forest, out of windows
torn from old farmhouses.

I lay them on the earth before painting the frames
turquoise and yellow and gray.

I mean to build you a memory house, to enact some voodoo
so you can come to just this place to remember my name,
my Girl Scout troop number, what I want to be when I grow up.

Apprehension compresses me, keeps me from showing you this place.
I sit for a while, listening in case you find it yourself.

I will sleep in here, beneath the impenetrable rain
that is your memory.

Three

Not Yet Bones

Somewhere a reporter trips a child, snaps a photo to call it suffering.

Here in this library, college lovers plan to change the world.

When my baby lost her tongue thrust, my mother found
it, fights the spoon as I offer ice cream and mashed potatoes.

I mean to ask my OB if it's her, my mother, whom I miscarried.

An Oil Texture

You are woven in deep reds on my back like an oil painting.
No, perhaps not the woman *in* the oil painting—a woman
of an oil painting. The folds of your forehead textured
the way the canvass feels as I run my hands across it.

I picture you often as a twenty-something college woman,
who proudly tells a prying aunt that you will never marry,
never carry a child. Your mouth turns round, like a Van Gough

while you laugh inside. You go on to study biomedical engineering,
shattering your 1980's destination of a community-college education.

I have many costumes for you.

Fleshed

Today, I have no connection with this plate, this meal.

A thousand cows come together in one hamburger.
        We are afraid to touch.

I'll spend hours spinning porcelain bowls to hold a carcass
who lived for hours.

Today: in an Island Chapel

He lies during his vows, is married, and presumably is not struck by lightening.

I taught writing this morning for the first time. When I asked my students to share their least favorite experience in school, Nadiman said *pass*, then wrote me a letter about his fifth-grade teacher who beat him in a closet in a Nigeran boys' school.

When I returned home, I rocked my sleeping infant after hearing a news report of a mother breaking her child's head in the bathtub.

Today: she remains encased, protected from all of this.

Turquoise

If I could hide
in your bookshelves
        I would crawl in between the pages
where I could walk with Heathcliff
        and Amy March.

I would let them tell me about you,
tell me what you hid from inside
        their stories.

A mother watched her boyfriend
beat her baby to death over
        the course of one day.

She sits in jail tonight, wanting to crawl
into the pages of Minnie Mouse
        on the baby's bookshelves.

And, all at the same time, a baby slipped from
a womb into a silent hospital room,
        nameless, and no book shelves.
        He should have had more time.

My womb is waiting for one more warm baby to fill it,
        but I am too afraid.

Unique Brain

As the polar ice caps melt, new marine life makes its way into the Arctic. The barriers that once kept orcas in warmer waters are gone.

As the mammal swims into the new temperatures, she seeks a lion seal.

But the water may freeze her unique brain. She will act odd, forget that she is part of a family pod.

Suddenly, she makes deeper dives. And the youngest one can't make it to the surface in time.

When I Knew you were Forgetting

It was the night of your niece's bachelorette party. I was nineteen and you were forty-eight. You picked me up at my apartment. On the way home, you insisted you had to drive, because I had one strawberry margarita. I spoke clearly the directions to you as we exited the highway, because you had trouble with that sometimes. It was our joke, your tendency to get lost over the years. This time was different though. *Go left off the exit, then right at the light. They changed the exit, remember? That construction project over the summer. You have to turn left now. Turn left. Okay, good. Now when this light turns green, go right. Mom, go right. Mom GO RIGHT.* You went straight and we were back on the highway. I was a selfish asshole still, and yelled, telling you there was something wrong with you. You need to see a doctor, I said. But you just stared and got off at the next exit.

Cathartic

A death slow
enough for
water to rise.

A life quick
enough to miss.

A child small
enough to hide.

Four

Turquoise

On the back of Alzheimer's patients' necks, there is a muscle
that will eventually tighten and stay constricted.
It will be so tight that no amount of coaxing while the patient
stares with one eye unseeing and one fixedly on your cheek will convince
her to release the grip on her brainstem for a wash in a shampoo bowl.

This will surprise the caretaker, on a trip to a nursing center's salon,
that suddenly something that we so wanted to hang onto for a sense
of normalcy is taken and piled in the closet with a filing box of unused
cards for all occasions that she kept for convenience.

Flowers. Fresh flowers can replace a weekly trip to the salon room.
They will last roughly two weeks, so every other Monday
now she can have this special treat instead to enjoy with a Diet Coke
only drunk from a straw.

A house plant could also encourage air to come back into the room.
Pile her room with plants and vegan cookies and detox drinks.
Wash the forgetting right out of her.

Spill

Twice now, you slip into an elevator in her dream,
and she nearly doesn't notice you.

Your lashes are as soft as she remembers.
Suddenly you tell her that today is not a bad
          speaking day.

So you talk for hours about everything you missed. She says,
          I have three children now, I'm not afraid
          of my body, I make clay bowls at my
          kitchen counter. When I write in my notebook,
          it's in your handwriting.

Then she says, *don't come back.*

Lost

When mother gets lost she stands on the sidewalk at Harrison's shopping center two miles away. She is with the fire station because they found her this time with the tracking device on her wrist. When mother gets lost she has her toes in the creek. When she is lost she's forgotten us, the ones who grew in her womb. She's forgotten our home, our cats, she's forgotten my children. When my mother gets lost she's left at night, her phone forgotten on the floor. She left in the morning, to look for her purse. Her hair shakes as she says to me, like a robin— *I'm so sorry, so sorry, so.* Her sorrys are really the calls of crows.

Turquoise

She came as a "T" signed in ink. When mother came back
she came as evenings at Cheesecake Factory and as a second
bread basket. She came back as pink tulip wallpaper.
When my mother came back she was turquoise. She had the same soft chin.
When my mother came back she came back childless. She came back alive.

Bad Mother

Rachel would sneak back into her aunt's house where her baby hid. She'd rock the baby, crawl out before morning no one knew. Until one morning the police flooded her kitchen, and the reporter couldn't speak when the camera said action outside her home, because no one knew the words for collecting a baby scattered throughout the first floor of a custom built two-story home. So the reporter stared into the camera man's face. Now Rachel's window's on the top floor of the locked hospital. The baby's father said he would try again, to find a baby that could be held together by light. I told him he could find some in California and hide them under my pillow.

Visit

I can't, today. I can't come to you today.
        My two daughters are ill from a virus they caught at a babysitter.
You would have been the one caring for them, but you're in your home now.
So I will stay here, and try to help them sleep at the same time,
        really so I can escape them.

I should come to you later today, but instead I may just wait
 in the parking spot outside your side window.
        You are gone.

Gone from your big white home with mauve walls and iced tea makers.
        You've been so long without iced tea, and I long for you to save me
from forgetting, from remembering, from mothering.

Headstone

When it's past 1:00 she knows if she hears a cry it's from her child,
not her mother. Mother is locked now in the section where dreams lie buried.
If Mother came back it would be through the rise of lucidity,
where a cut above her cheek was visible and she could still recite the president.

Her son recites the presidents and learns cursive now.
He hangs on her arms and her brainstem and reminds her
how to not forget about lunchroom bartering—how he had traded fruit for Doritos.

He doesn't know, she had read that packing extra fruit and vegetables
could save him from Alzheimer's when he is gray.

Those *apples are to help you remember your kids one day,*
she whispers from the front seat.

Five

Night Rise

I long for the night where the body of your house takes you back.
And I will be able to see who you could be today.

Without drool and with memories,
the dreams taunt me,
        call it teasing.
Show me who you'd be.

Now I wake to children crying. My husband is away
so I lay in coffee and imagination,
waiting for you to wake.

Every Way You've Died

You died the first time I had to lock your apartment
from the outside, so you wouldn't wander the streets.

After the police found you, and your neighbor found you,
and you were waitlisted for homes. I researched if I would go to jail
for leaving you so I could work and nurse my baby.

You died when you told me about your husband who didn't exist.
He'd been gone for years and years, but to you he was a doctor
who would punish me for keeping you inside.

You died when we ran out of money for medication
and your hallucinations were worse. I spent time seeing
if I could find them in Canada for you.

You really died when I walked into an ER with you,
telling the nurses you couldn't be alone anymore.

I visited every day, and every day you asked
if you could come home now.

And every time I said no, not yet, I helped kill you.

Rainforest Depletion

It's all alive, and it's dead. Fucking is dead. Our food is dead, our forks are dead, our lives are dead, the president is dead, the neighbors are dead, our children are dead, orcas and 150 year old turtles are dead, floating in the water. The roads are dead, the movies theaters are dead, the sun is dead, the water is dead, your coffee is dead, your Gods are dead, the books are dead, the trees are dead. Music is dead. Our skin is dead, our phones are dead, your pens and paint brushes. Meryl Streep and donuts. Color and virginity and feminism are dead. Promises and families and education and pain. The dead feed on us and we feed on the dead.

Play

I should get caught up on children's baby books before my womb fills again.

Today, I decided to be a teacher.

That way I would spend my days with children and learn how to keep mine alive.

My children wouldn't know that you are gone if they could watch me make construction stencils.

There's a square of concrete at the bus stop, where I imagine you stand.

I return home to break dishes, to walk a park trail,

to pretend.

Jungle

A silence strong enough to climb.

Clay and Hips and Jungles

Today, I learn about jungles that swallow bulldozers when the loggers leave at night. I hear the story on the radio as I mold clay into the shape of your hips.

These hips that you said you wanted to be seen but not heard. I never really asked you what that meant.

      This might be the belief that chipped away at you for decades.

I'm trying to teach my hips to make more sound, but still end in a quick death, rather than the intermittent one that you're dying, the kind that starts and stops—

a slaughterhouse operating during a summer storm.

Asphyxiation by Bulimia in October

I long for straight rows of all purple flowers that reach across miles.
  A place where your nursing home could be.

Only when I'm stopped at the sign to your entrance do I notice a car-sized spider
cross the road. Is it looking for you, too?

I long to tell you that I've been able to heal, to beat away
the part of me who needed a cycle of emptying and filling.

That part grew again, though. And I haven't the strength
  to cut it back tonight.

She's Where Babies Come From

My mother grows on every surface.
She is in the crack under my front door,
the folds of my bathroom towels, the dimple
of this new baby's chin.

She lives in the pavement outside
the home, seeped into a wooden fence post, pours from the bottoms
of potted petunias.

I think she escaped through the lock on her ward to flood my world.

Six

Caretaker

A young boy kissed his mother goodbye in her bed.
He found her cold.

She had been gone for hours, but her arms were open.
He laid in them for a while, then went to school.
When he came home he finished his homework, T.V., macaroni.

He drug his sleeping bag into the mother's room and slept
on the floor next to her.

He repeated the process for days, adding in baseball practice
and paying cash at the deli for milk and chips.

On Saturday he watched cartoons all day and folded her socks. Sunday he went
to church and had two peanut butter sandwiches for dinner before reading *Harry Potter* aloud.

When it was time to go to school on Monday, he stopped into the front office to
let them know.

The World, Now that It's Quiet

She bought the new journal herself, with a basket of Cosmo flowers to hang above the patio table where she sips her coffee after letting it sit for too long. An expired marriage license collected dust on the ironing board in a spare bedroom. She remembered it as she dipped her hands in the water, unrolled the clay, slammed it on the canvas table. She wondered what justification is there in being an indignant wife, except she did not know she was one until the mistress phoned. She may allow herself a few days to wallow. She unrolls the clay, not using the wheel this time. Her radio said, *The world is in the midst of a porcelain revolution*—Yes, how true, she thinks, without really knowing what she means.

Bad Mother

Someone named Gail is on the news. She carried baby Molly through the hospital. Security asked her if she needed help. *My baby's dead*, she told him. And Molly was dead. The coroner stopped counting the cigarette burns, the bruises too. That night I dreamt I found Molly under the creek rocks. I nursed her. When I woke, sixteen articles had appeared. I read them all. *Gail was home with three of her eight children, the other five in foster care, number nine on the way.* I want number nine. How can I steal number nine? I still look for Gail. I know her street. I know Molly lived in a bathtub. Molly sometimes left through the drain to wait for me by the creek.

An Interruption of the Fanaticism

After the game I became a crop, harvested when guilt needed to be sponged. My father told me they were finally tearing down the public housing near his apartment. It brings down the value of the neighborhood. We rode past the building once, watched a young girl carry groceries inside from the bus stop. That's a rough place to grow up, he had said. I wondered what will happen to the child when she returned from her grocery trip to a wrecking ball.

When my father lost me in Wal-Mart I stopped looking and waited by the bicycles until he came back around.

A Slow Decay

I wonder, what if I stay here, forever
        alive.

Long after the husband, children, cat—died.

I'll have forgotten them, but I'll stay rooted
to this memory house.

Death decays at my mother, starting with unused
parts of the brain stem while the rest
goes on.

Death by Distraction

As I drive through city traffic I thought about what it will mean if cancer
or a bus kills me while I wait for Alzheimer's to find me.

If I spend so much time hiding from the act of losing memories
I'll forget to look out for murderers and pic axes.

This will surely drown me, a death of fear.

Waves

Today, I forgot that the street to your nursing home
crosses my alternate route.

The wave comes swiftly, suddenly.
It breaks me, empties me.

It washes me to the memory house where I search
for you under floorboards and ominous fact.

It carries me further from you, to where you can't hold
my babies, serve as the surrogate for what I cannot ever
be. This lifetime will surely be the one of regret.

Picnic Mother

Today, I wake after my dream of you waiting for the yellow bus to return. You had prepared the backyard picnic that would become a kindergarten tradition. This has become the memory to which my mothering tools are always compared. I think of the pink and purple picnic basket when I imagine myself, one day, writing your obituary. Suddenly the dream changes and I'm giving your eulogy, slumped over a podium in front of a crowd of purple mourners without any words coming. Just standing still. Again, the dream changes. It wakes me suddenly. And I realize that you will remain ever awake—but at the same time, you will remain even more dead.

Unfinished

Sleepless, I imagine you telling me, *when you mother, we mother,*
as if you've passed, and now you live inside of me.
It eases me, until I realize it isn't true.

> That we can't mother, with you still living outside of me.
> Because you are not dead.

You erode, continually, slipping to the point of death, then crawl back again.

I think you've been trying to die now for years. You may take me with you.

Imprint

I go to our big white house in my dreams.
       It's empty as I look through the windows.

When I lean on the door, I slip through, walk through the rooms of memory.

Our living room still has the same railing and your bathroom door still sticks.
       My small bedroom fills with you when I enter.

The same shelf was broken in the closet, the same mirrors hung on the door.

In the kitchen I saw our years of solitary meals, when we were the only
ones left in this hallow place.

I settle on the tiles you spent weeks selecting.
       I decide to stay in one place.

I'll wait for you here.

Memorization

Today, I forgot my keys.
>(Naturally I'm now afraid of forgetting my children too.)

I remember sitting in a hospital bed as I memorized their newborn faces,
>burning their noses and lips into my brain.

Surely, this is impossible to forget, I think.

Bad Mother

Maura's little cousin found Baby Ben on the counter, and Maura sleeping in the back room. They were hours too late. The call to the police was inaudible with screams and I had to stop the recording of the 911 call, start it again. Stop. Start. The screams are inside of me now. Maura was every mother who is bad for not taking her medicines, for skipping appointments, but is able to smile with lipstick when the social worker comes to the door. I could sneak into the morgue and put Ben together once more, wrap him on my back, and carry him away from numb horror to a pool of forgetting.

Seven

Water Calls

In every corner of my bag I keep you hidden with me. I try to not drop you during
the day.

> But at a dock in Santa Barbara, I plan to drop you into the water,
> watch you drift into a place among grandmother orcas
> teaching daughters to nurse their calves.

I want to be somewhere where I won't see your clear hazel eyes in my sister's face.

Maybe Ireland or the Gibbon Islands where I can learn to swim better and shark-
call.

> But you will lure me home. I'm sure of it.

If I Found You in Gulf Shores

We cannot collect or categorize your memories. You're left in the swift turning of pages on my bookshelves and receipt keeping.

Dorsal fins break the surface and I think I can throw myself from the balcony where I sit and find you in the water.

Escaped from the permanent ward of internment, you wait for me there, and I can be the child again.

Nana

To my girls, you are a fairytale. They wonder who I came from.
So I tell them of the woman who has special helpers that buy their birthdays gifts.
Her little fairies watch you, she knows that you love ponies, and that you love paints.

From the corner, my oldest watches, knowing the truth.
When I feel brave, we all come to your home,
close the door to your room, pretend.

I'm afraid that your decay could taint the story of you.
Mostly we pretend that you are not an omen.

The oldest plays along, because he can remember you before this home
when you played with him, when you knew his name.

When they seem afraid of you he tells the girls, *Nana's fairies bought me this book.*

Surrogate

I think of you as the mother
who is trapped in a bathtub
with a collapsing dorsal fin,

after her daughter is
taken during the night
by a craned sling.

You fight for that baby,
using the long-range vocals
in search of her.

But your daughter is quiet that night,
not knowing how to answer the calls.

Weeks later, she kills her trainer,
dragging the body slowly to the floor,

to the surface,
to the floor again.

Slip

I look for you again in the vacant childhood home.
Through the latched gate, beyond a barren vegetable garden.

After standing for a while on the back deck,
I descend to stand at the pool's edge.

Here I look into my childhood, drowned.
You could have let yourself sink below here after a bottle
of wine and pockets of rocks.

You could have slipped through the filter, saved yourself.

Afternoon Garden

A bee pollinates my memory house.
You lived here with me once. Now it's empty save
for the noise of rolling purple water on the walls.

Outside pansies are pulled apart, then planted
in separate forgetting holes. There is soft
noise on the plexiglass bases of clouds.

Ink runs from the garden hose, your fingerprints
permeate clay pots that you spun, and puddles of lipstick
collect under the ladder nailed to a tree.

Kristina **Nichole Brodbeck**'s work has been published or isforthcoming in *The Cape Rock, For a Better World 2017* and *2018, Calliope,* and *The Oddville Press. Play* is her first collection. This collection first began as individual poems in Kelly Moffett's poetry workshop as part of the Northern Kentucky University MAE program, then grew into her thesis project prior to graduation. She maintains a blog at kristinanicholebrodbeck.wordpress.com where she writes in reflection of the creative process, popular culture, and current events. She lives in Cincinnati, Ohio with her husband, Ryan, and their three children: Owen, Rosalie, and Aurora. She thanks Ryan for his endless encouragement and willingness to step away from a scientific mindset and into the realm of poetic process to serve as a reader for this collection. She is an Adjunct Professor at Mount St. Joseph University and Cincinnati State.

CPSIA information can be obtained
at www.ICGtesting.com
Printed in the USA
LVHW041505040919
629924LV00012B/1216